William Humphrey

The Vicar of Christ

William Humphrey

The Vicar of Christ

ISBN/EAN: 9783/42897558

Manufactured in Europe, USA, Canada, Australia, Japa

Cover: Foto ©Lupo / pixelio.de

Manufactured and distributed by brebook publishing software (www.brebook.com)

William Humphrey

The Vicar of Christ

THE VICAR OF CHRIST

BY

THE REV. WILLIAM HUMPHREY, S. J.

LONDON AND LEAMINGTON
Art and Book Company
NEW YORK, CINCINNATI AND CHICAGO
BENZIGER BROTHERS
1892

PREFACE.

The following pages are reprinted from *The Month*, by kind permission of the Editor.

The purpose of the writer is to press home on his readers four truths:—

1. That Jesus Christ, the Incarnate Son of God, has a visible Kingdom on this earth.
2. That in this Kingdom He not only reigns, but *rules*.
3. That His rule, both in teaching and in government, is rendered actual by means of that man whom He has made to be His Vicar on this earth.
4. And that, if Christ had no visible Vicar, His royalty would be merely nominal and not real.

WILLIAM HUMPHREY, S.J.

CATHOLIC CHURCH, OXFORD,
Feast of St. Ignatius, 1892.

CONTENTS.

I.

THE VICAR OF CHRIST.

	PAGE
THE IDEA OF A VICAR	4
SIMON MADE TO BE PETER (THE ROCK) ...	5
THE CHURCH AS IT IS A HOUSE WITH ITS FOUNDATION—A SOCIETY WITH ITS CENTRAL AUTHORITY	8
CHRIST AS HE IS HIMSELF THE ROCK ...	10
THE KEYS OF THE KINGDOM	11
BINDING AND LOOSING	13
PETER THE CONFIRMER OF HIS BRETHREN ...	15
THE SUPREME AND UNIVERSAL PASTOR	19
PERPETUITY OF THE PRIMACY ...	24
SUCCESSORS OF PETER	27
MODE OF THEIR SUCCESSION	28

II.

THE VICAR OF CHRIST IN HIS RELATION TO THE CHURCH OF CHRIST.

PERPETUITY OF THE CHURCH OF CHRIST ...	33
PERPETUITY OF THE VICAR OF CHRIST ...	34
THE CHURCH AS BUILT BY CHRIST HIMSELF	36

DIVINE LAW—ECCLESIASTICAL LAW	39
THE CHURCH AS IT IS THE BODY OF CHRIST	40
CHRIST'S VICAR, AS ITS VISIBLE HEAD ...	41
HIS JURISDICTION—ORDINARY—IMMEDIATE ...	44
UNIVERSAL BISHOP—BISHOP OF BISHOPS ...	47
BISHOPS OF DIVINE INSTITUTION—PRINCES— PASTORS	51
APPEALS TO THE VICAR OF CHRIST	54
CHRIST, THE DIVINE TEACHER	56
INFALLIBILITY OF HIS VICAR	58
UTTERANCES "EX CATHEDRA"	59
CONVOCATION OF COUNCILS	61
EMPERORS AND COUNCILS	63
RIGHT OF CHRIST'S VICAR TO PRESIDE ...	65
BISHOPS, AS JUDGES OF FAITH	66
PROCEDURE—EXAMINATION—SUFFRAGE ...	67
PONTIFICAL DEFINITIONS—CONCILIAR DEFINITIONS	71
NO APPEAL FROM THE PONTIFF TO A COUNCIL	73
MONARCHY OF THE CHURCH	74
VACANCIES OF THE VICAR'S CHAIR	75

III.

THE VICAR OF CHRIST IN HIS RELATION TO CIVIL SOCIETY.

CIVIL SOCIETY—CIVIL GOVERNMENT—CIVIL POWER	79

IMMEDIATE END OF THE CIVIL RULER ...	82
RELATION OF CIVIL TO RELIGIOUS POWER ...	83
DIRECT AND INDIRECT SUBORDINATION ...	84
CHURCH AND STATE	86
CONCORDATS—ORIGIN—ESSENTIAL CHARACTER —OBLIGATION — INTERPRETATION —REVOCATION	87
ROYAL PLACETS, OR EXEQUATURS	92
PERSONAL IMMUNITY OF CHRIST'S VICAR NOT OF ECCLESIASTICAL — OR CIVIL — BUT OF DIVINE LAW	96
MUST BE STABLE—AND MANIFEST	99
HIS CIVIL PRINCEDOM—ITS NECESSITY ...	101

THE VICAR OF CHRIST.

AMONG the many titles of the Roman Pontiff, there is no one which so sets forth that Pontiff's place in the Christian economy as does his title of *Vicar of Christ*.

The Roman Pontiff is rightly called the visible Head of the visible Church; but to ascertain all that is implied in this title, we must first have determined what that Church is.

The Roman Pontiff is the Successor of Peter, the Prince of the Apostles; but to ascertain what that is to which he has succeeded, we must first have determined the privilege of Peter, and the status of the Apostles.

The Roman Pontiff is Universal Bishop, and the Bishop of Bishops; but to ascertain the nature of the power which this title denotes, we must first have determined what a Bishop is.

The Roman Pontiff is the immediate Pastor—the Teacher and Ruler of all the faithful of the flock of Christ; but to ascertain what his pastoral functions are, we must first have determined what that flock is.

There are, it is true, certain advantages in commencing consideration of the place of the Roman Pontiff in the Christian economy with this last question, Who are the faithful of the flock of Christ? and ascending to the questions, What are Bishops? What were the Apostles? and What was the relation of Peter to them? But, for some purposes at least, there are still greater advantages in beginning with consideration of Peter in his direct relation to Jesus Christ. We have then to put to ourselves one previous question only—the question which Christ put to Peter—"Whom do you say that I, the Son of Man, am?" If we can answer with Peter, "Thou art the Christ, the Son of the living God," we can proceed at once to consider the action of Christ on Peter, which put Peter in Christ's place as His Vicar and Vicegerent.

When we profess with Peter that Jesus of Nazareth is the Son of the living God, we express our faith in His personal divinity—that Jesus is a divine Person, and the Son of another divine Person, who is God the Father. When we say with Peter that Jesus is the Christ, we express our faith in His divine Mission—that He, the Incarnate Son of God, was sent by God the Father, and anointed with the Holy Ghost to teach men—to sanctify and to offer sacrifice for men—and to rule and govern men with divine authority.

This was the three-fold purpose of the mission and advent of Jesus, as He was the Christ. This is the three-fold work which He was sent and came to do, which He did while He dwelt visibly in the midst of men, and which He is doing now by means of the ministry of men, with whom He is all days, as He foretold and promised, to the end of the world, in the person of him whom He has made to be His Vicar upon earth.

The idea of a *Vicar*, as the name implies, involves the closest relation between two persons, between the vicar and him of whom he is the vicar. A vicar is put in the place of him whom he represents. He is invested with his power, he is furnished with his authority, or as much thereof as is necessary for the doing of those acts for the sake of which he is made vicar. He personates his principal. If his principal is a king, the vicar of that king is a viceroy. The vicar is a servant, but he is the *alter ego* of his master. The two persons are morally one in their action, and the acts of the vicar are morally acts of his master. The vicar's acts lay the same weight of obligation on the master's subjects as do the acts of the master himself. The master, by his appointment of a vicar, binds himself to ratify his vicar's acts, and to recognize them as his own.

The vicar has close relations with his master's subjects, but those relations are not so close as is his own relation to his master. Master and vicar stand apart, and as if they stood alone—and in this relation we find Jesus of Nazareth and Simon of

Bethsaida standing on the day when Jesus put the question, "Whom do you say that I am?"

The question was put to the disciples, but the answer was given by Simon, and thereafter all the words of Jesus on that occasion are addressed to Simon, singularly and individually, as if those two had been there alone together.

Simon's answer, "Thou art the Christ, the Son of the living God," was a profession made by him as an individual of his own faith. He did not speak as the spokesman of the other disciples. He was not their delegate, and he was not expressing in their name that which he knew to be their belief. Simon spoke for himself alone.

This is clear from the words of Jesus, which declare that there had been an immediate manifestation by the Eternal Father to Simon individually of the truth of the personal divinity and divine mission of Jesus. This divine revelation to Simon was the cause of his faith in the truth revealed, and of his profession of that faith. His faith, and his profession of it, were the effect of that revelation. The three combined—the revelation by the Father to Simon individually—his individual faith therein—and his individual profession thereof—formed the reason why he individually was declared by Jesus to be *blessed*. " Blessed *art thou*, Simon Bar-Jona, because flesh and blood hath not revealed it *to thee*, but My Father who is in Heaven."

Jesus said to Simon in effect, As My Father hath manifested My personal divinity and divine mission *to thee*, and as *thou* hast believed in it, and hast professed it, so do I now make known to thee and declare thine own individual destiny and dignity. And so He continues, " And I say *to thee* that *thou art* Peter."

Jesus did not say, Thou art Peter, and on Myself I will build My Church. Nor are His words susceptible of this meaning. To read into them any such meaning would be to empty the name of Peter bestowed on Simon of all its significance, and to turn that which was given by way of privilege and pledge of a singular blessedness into a mockery of Simon.

It was not the first time that Jesus had spoken to Simon individually, and in connection with this name of Peter. On the day when Andrew, having heard John the Baptist give testimony to Jesus, and declare Him to be the Lamb of God, sought out his brother Simon, and said to him, "We have found the Messias, the Christ," and brought him to Jesus, Jesus looking upon Simon said, "Thou art Simon the son of Jona, thou shalt be called Cephas, which is interpreted Peter." That which Jesus then foretold and promised, He now fulfils. In the desert of Jordan He said, "Thou *shalt be called* Peter." In the confines of Cæsarea Philippi He said, "*Thou art* Peter."

The name of *Peter* imposed on Simon was not merely a name, as was his name of Simon. It signified that which Christ had made him to be. He now was that which his new name signifies— the Rock. Imposition of a name by God effects that which the name signifies. When the Incarnate God said to Simon, "Thou art Peter," it was equivalent to his saying, Thou art the Rock. So saying, He made him to be that Rock to which He refers when He continues, "And upon this Rock I will build My Church."

Two things have now been declared by Jesus: first, that Simon has been made by Him the Rock; and secondly, that He intends to build upon that Rock a Church which shall be His. It is manifest, therefore, that the relation of Peter to the future Church of Christ is the same as is the relation of a foundation to the house which is built upon it. As the house is here the Church, and as Christ is the Architect and Builder of that house, so is Peter the Rock on which, as on its foundation, the Church is laid and rests.

There is nothing which is more necessary to a house than is its foundation. On the stability of the foundation depends the permanence of the house. Further, there are two things which are of the intrinsic idea of a foundation, or two things which are necessary to a foundation as such: one is, that the foundation must remain supporting the house, as long as the house itself endures—the other is, that no part of the house can exist outside or beyond the foundation on which the house is laid. It follows that in the Christian economy Peter must have his place as the Rock on which the Church rests, as long as the Church itself endures. It follows also that any building which does not rest as on its foundation on the living Rock of Peter, is not, and cannot be, a part of the one Church of Christ. *Ubi Petrus, ibi Ecclesia*— "Where Peter is, there is the Church."

The Church of Christ was to be a visible society of living men. That which is to every society what a foundation is to the house that is built upon it, is the central and supreme authority which constitutes it as a society, and by which it is ruled and governed. This authority is the principle of its stability and of its unity. When Jesus therefore made one man to be the living Rock on which He was to build the society of living men which is His Church on earth, He invested that one man with supreme authority over that society.

That society was to endure for ever. Jesus said, "And the gates of Hell shall not prevail against it." And this He said in immediate connection with His previous words, "Thou art Peter (the Rock), and on this Rock I will build My Church." The gates of Hell are Satan and his satellites, and among them the children of unbelief and disobedience, and Peter, as he is the living and lasting Rock, is the cause why they shall not prevail against the Church of Christ, which rests on him.

But was not Christ Himself the living Rock on which His Church is built? He was undoubtedly, and it is just because He was and is the Rock, that Peter—as made by Christ to be the Rock—is manifestly Christ's Vicar on the earth. Christ is the principal Rock. Peter is the Rock by communication and participation. Christ associated and, in a manner, identified Peter with Himself as He is the Rock. He thus made Peter to be His Vicar in all that concerns His own Primacy and Headship. As Vicar of Christ Peter was to be the principle of stability—the centre of unity—and the source of jurisdiction for the whole of that society of living men which Jesus calls *My Church*.

2

That there should be no mistake as to His meaning, Jesus now changes the metaphor, and presents the same idea under other words. He speaks of His Church as a Kingdom, and says to Peter individually and in the singular, " I will give *to thee* the keys of the Kingdom of Heaven."

The giving of keys is an undoubted sign and pledge of the imparting of a power. Giving of the keys of a house is a sign of right and power over that house, and over that which it contains. The keys of a kingdom signify royal power and supremacy of jurisdiction.

Christ, who is the principal Rock of His Church, is also the supreme Head or Monarch of that Church, which is His Kingdom upon the earth. As He had made Peter to be His Vicar, as He is the Rock, so was He to make Peter to be His Vicar, as He is King in His visible Kingdom.

This He was to do, not by abdicating, or by divesting Himself of His royalty, but by associating and, in a manner, identifying Peter with Himself in that royalty. So doing, He should do two things. He would invest Peter with supremacy of jurisdiction in His Kingdom, which is the Church; and He would exempt him from all dependence on his subjects. The Viceroy was to depend on and to be answerable to his Sovereign, but he was neither to depend on, nor to be judged by any one, or by the majority, or by all of his subjects.

The power to be conveyed by the giving of the keys of the Kingdom was the same as the power signified by making Peter to be the Rock; but the idea of the Kingdom more fully unfolds the rights and functions of him who is the living Rock.

Some of these, moreover, Jesus specified. He said to Peter, "Whatsoever thou shalt bind upon earth, it shall be bound also in Heaven; and whatsoever thou shalt loose upon earth, it shall be loosed also in Heaven."

Binding and loosing in the moral order signify imposing or releasing from moral obligation. Such power to bind and loose includes *legislative* power, or power to make laws; *judicial* power, or power to give sentence, and to carry it out; and power of *release*, by abrogation or dispensation of laws, and by remission of penalties incurred. It comprehends all the rights of supreme jurisdiction which are necessary for the well-ordering and right ruling and prosperous administration of a common-wealth.

This power bestowed on Peter was universal, as is manifest from the word *whatsoever*. It comprehends the binding and loosing of every thing whatsoever which in any way concerns the Kingdom of Christ upon the earth. Those things alone are not comprehended under it which are in no way connected with that Kingdom.

The power to bind and loose is not to be confounded with the power to forgive sins. The latter power was given to all the Apostles along with Peter, when Jesus said to them: "Receive ye the Holy Ghost; whose sins you shall forgive, they are forgiven them, and whose sins you shall retain, they are retained." The power to bind and loose was first given to Peter singly and alone, and it extended not merely to the forgiveness of sins, but to all things *whatsoever* which concern the Kingdom of the Church. It is true that the same words of bestowal of this power were afterwards addressed to all the Apostles along with Peter, but they were first addressed to Peter individually. This fact would be of itself sufficient to show that the power bestowed on them to bind and loose was bestowed on them as they together formed one society of which Peter was the head, and that they possessed it therefore with dependence on Peter. But the proof of this is still stronger. The place of the living Rock, on which the whole of the Church was to rest, and the keys of the Kingdom, were both alike given to Peter alone. They were never given to the rest of the Apostles. "*Thou art* Peter," and "*To thee* will I give the keys," were words said to Peter only. The giving of the keys signifies something more than is signified by bestowal of power to bind and loose. It includes the latter power which is contained in it as in its source and principle, and which, when bestowed on the other Apostles, was bestowed on them with dependence on him who had the power of the keys. In other words, the idea of possession of the keys includes two things—the power to bind and loose—and this power, in a supreme degree, and without dependence on any other. The power of the keys of the Kingdom is, in the Sacred Scriptures, ascribed to two persons only, to Jesus, and to Peter—to Christ the King, and to the Vicar of Christ.

3

On another occasion Jesus again addressed Peter singly and individually. He said to him: "Simon, Simon, Satan hath desired to have *you* (in the plural, *i.e.*, the Apostles), that he may sift you as wheat, but I have prayed *for thee*, that *thy faith* fail not, and *thou*, being once converted, confirm *thy brethren.*"

Here there can be no doubt that Peter alone is addressed. Not only does the repeated use of the personal pronoun in the singular designate one person, who is also addressed by his own individual name, but that person is separated from and opposed to the others, as the person confirming to the persons to be confirmed.

Jesus sets forth the design of Satan to be accomplished in the dispersion of the Apostles through the overthrow of their faith, and in connection therewith He speaks of His own prayer, not for them, but for Peter. He did not pray that the faith of the Apostles should not fail, but He did pray that the faith of Peter should not fail.

The unfailing faith of the one Peter was to be the source of the stability of the faith of the other Apostles. Jesus was Himself the Confirmer of His Apostles in their faith, as He was Himself the living Rock on which His Church was founded, and as He was Himself the holder of the keys of His Kingdom; but Simon, whom He had made to be Peter (the Rock), and to whom He was to give the keys of the Kingdom, was to be His Vicar in this also, that he was to occupy the place of Jesus in confirming his brethren in their faith.

The idea of confirmation of others includes dependence on the part of the persons confirmed, and independence of them on the part of him who confirms them. The Vicar of Christ, who was to confirm his brethren, should be ever dependent on Him of whom he was the Vicar, and whose efficacious prayer was the cause of his unfailing faith, but he would be in no way dependent on those who were in dependence on him.

Unfailing faith is infallibility—or immunity from error in matters of faith—and confirmation with unfailing faith is exercise of the office of an infallible teacher. To his right to confirm his brethren, there corresponds on their part, as they are his subjects, the duty of submitting themselves to be confirmed by him. Hence the necessity of the personal infallibility of him who is divinely charged to confirm his brethren in their faith. If he were not infallible, those who had been divinely made dependent on him might be led astray through the very fidelity of their obedience. If his faith were not unfailing, their obedience in dependence would lead them into the error into which he himself had fallen, and Satan would have his desire in their being sifted as wheat in the overthrow of their faith. There is the same necessity for the permanence of a Confirmer of his brethren in the Church of Christ, as there is for the permanence of the living Rock on which it rests. As the foundation must remain as long as the house that is built thereon endures, so must there remain a Confirmer of faith as long as the assaults of Satan for the overthrow of faith endure, and these will continue to the end of time.

The office and right of a Vicar of Christ to confirm his brethren in the faith is essential to the idea of that Church of Christ against which the gates of Hell are never to prevail.

4

On a third occasion did Jesus single out Simon and address him individually and by name. It was after His resurrection from the dead, and before His departure from the earth. He said to him: "Simon, son of John, lovest *thou* Me more than do these?" Again Simon is separated from the other Apostles by comparison with them, and it is manifest that the words of Jesus apply to him alone. Simon answered the question put to him, with the words, "Yea, Lord, Thou knowest that I love Thee;" and Jesus said to him, "Feed My lambs." A second time did He put to Simon the same question, and addressing him again by name, "Simon, son of John, lovest *thou* Me?" and receiving again the same answer, He repeated His charge, "Feed My lambs." A third time He put the question in the same words, and when Simon, being grieved because He said to him the third time, "Lovest *thou* Me," answered, "Lord, Thou knowest that I love Thee," Jesus said to him, "Feed My sheep."

Jesus had on a previous occasion said of Himself, "I am the Good Shepherd," and He had spoken of His sheep. His sheep are those who believe in and follow Him. He now puts Peter in His place as Pastor, and as supreme and universal Pastor of the whole of His flock. Peter is to feed not only the lambs of Christ's fold, but those also who have begotten them again unto God. The words of Jesus are universal and without exception or restriction. He says not only, "Feed My lambs," but "Feed My sheep."

Peter had once exalted himself above the other Apostles in his profession of his love for Jesus, and, with reference to his subsequent fall, Jesus now questions him as to whether he really loves Him with that special love which he had then professed to have. Peter could not possibly have known whether he in reality excelled the other Apostles in his love, and when Jesus asked him, it was not to learn this from him, but to show how great a lover of Christ a Vicar of Christ ought to be. He put His questions, not to upbraid Peter, but to draw from him a profession of his excellence of love. Taken in connection with these questions, His command, "Feed My sheep," testifies to His knowledge of the reality of the special excellence of Peter's love.

From Peter alone did Jesus exact, before bestowal of office, some special disposition of faith or charity, as from one whom He was about to endow with special privileges and prerogatives. Before He made him to be the living Rock, He drew from him a profession of faith in His personal Divinity, as revealed to him by the Eternal Father. Before He makes him to be the supreme Pastor of all the faithful, He draws from him a profession of his love.

On Peter, along with other disciples, had already

been bestowed divine mission and apostolic power, for to the Twelve Jesus had said, "As the Father hath sent Me, I also send you," but over and above this mission and power, there is now bestowed on him alone, and not on them, the office and right of feeding all the faithful of the flock of Christ. Peter's special love was a fitting disposition for this special office, and his reward was as special as was his love. It was something over and above the apostolic office, and this could only be that primacy of jurisdiction over his fellow-Apostles, as well as over all the faithful, which must belong to that man who is the Vicar of Christ.

This primacy of jurisdiction had most certainly been *promised* at Cæsarea Philippi, when to him who was then made to be the living Rock, it was said, "I will give *to thee* the keys of the Kingdom of Heaven,"—and this promise then made was now *fulfilled*.

In like manner was now fulfilled the prediction that in his unfailing faith he should be the Confirmer of his brethren, for he who, by his teaching and ruling with Divine authority, feeds all the faithful, confirms them in their faith and following of that Divine Shepherd of whom he is the Vicar.

The Apostles, who were sheep of the flock of Christ, were foundations of the Church of Christ, but they were foundations laid on one living Rock. They were pastors of the lambs, but under him to whom alone the charge was given to feed both the sheep and the lambs of Christ,—who rests on no other rock save Christ,—who receives no keys save from the hands of Christ—and who is confirmed in his faith by no one save by Christ Himself.

When the foundation shall rest upon its superstructure, when the fallible shall confirm the infallible, and when the sheep shall feed their shepherd, then may we entertain the idea that the Vicar of Christ may be dependent on, and answerable to any man who is not the Christ and the Son of the living God.

When Jesus declared His purpose to build a Church, and to build it upon a Rock, He spoke of that Church in the singular, and as one. He thus indicated that He has a Church on earth, and that one Church alone upon the earth is His.

To Simon, whom He had made to be the living Rock, when He said to him, "*Thou art* Peter" (the Rock), He foretold His purpose of the future when He added, "And on this Rock I will build *My Church.*"

All that which Peter was then made to be in the one Church of Christ, must remain and exist in the Church to-day, if it is that one Church which Jesus founded.

This is as certain and as manifest as it is certain and manifest that the foundation of a house must remain as long as the house itself endures. A foundation may remain when the house has fallen, but before the foundation can be removed, the house which was built upon it must have been overthrown.

When a society has been constituted by the establishment within it of a supreme authority as the centre of its unity and the source of its stability and the principle of its action, the society may be dissolved by rebellion, while the authority remains intact; but if the authority is withdrawn, the society as such must cease to be.

The endurance to the end of time of that visible society of living men, which is the one Church of Christ upon the earth, is guaranteed by the words of Christ. The permanence in that society of a man who is Christ's Vicar upon earth is equally guaranteed. Without a Vicar of Christ upon the earth there cannot exist upon the earth that Church of Christ in which He established one man as His Vicar, as He did when He made Peter (the Rock) to be the keeper of the keys of the Kingdom, the Confirmer of his brethren, and the supreme Pastor of all the faithful.

Among the component parts and constituent elements of the Church of Christ, there is no one which is of such paramount importance as is the perpetuity of the Primacy which was first constituted in Simon Peter. It is of cardinal importance, for on it the perpetuity of the Church of Christ hinges.

Apart from the perpetuity of a Vicar of Christ, the Church of Christ would have lost its identity. It would not be the same Church as that which Jesus founded. In that Church he placed a man whom He had made to be His Vicar,—or, to be more strictly accurate, upon a man whom He had made to be His Vicar He established His Church, as upon the stable foundation of a living and lasting Rock.

It is certain that Simon Peter lives no longer upon the earth. It is as certain that the Church of Christ exists upon the earth to-day. It is equally certain that the primacy established in Peter, as Vicar of Christ, is as much the foundation of the visible Church in this century as it was the foundation of the Church in the first age of its existence.

As the first members of the visible Church of Christ who have passed away have their successors in the living members who compose that society to-day, so has the first visible Head of the Church of Christ his successor in a living man, who is to-day as much the Vicar of Christ as was Simon Peter when Jesus ascended into Heaven. Peter has had, has, and must have his successors in the primacy. His successors are many in number, but the primacy is one, as the Church itself is one, although generation after generation has passed away of the millions of members who composed it while they were alive upon the earth.

As the primacy was not of the institution of the Church, but of the institution of Christ, so the perpetuity of the primacy depends not on the will of the Church, but on the will of Christ. It is not of ecclesiastical law; it is, equally with the primacy itself, of divine law.

Given the divine law of the perpetuity of a series of successors of St. Peter, as he was Vicar of Christ, there can be no doubt as to who his successor is. Men have denied the divine institution of the primacy, but the primacy as Vicar of Christ over the whole Church has never been claimed by, or supposed to belong to any one who was not the Bishop of Rome. Men have denied his claim, but no man has ever claimed the primacy in place of him. It is only through the Roman Bishopric that St. Peter can have successors. That Bishopric he held till the day of his death. In the words of the Vatican Council, he founded that See, and consecrated it with his blood. With it the right to the primacy is bound up. Whosoever is Bishop of Rome, and thus successor of St. Peter in that See, is successor of St. Peter also in the primacy.

It might happen that at some time there should be doubt as to the individual who had right to the Bishopric of Rome, or as to who was really the Bishop of Rome, but there can never be doubt that he who is Bishop of Rome is also the Vicar of Christ.

If a primacy in the Church had been instituted by the Church, it would have been a primacy, indeed, but it would not have been the primacy which was instituted by Jesus Christ in Peter. He who held it would not have been either Vicar of Christ or successor of St. Peter. His primacy would have rested on merely ecclesiastical law, and not on divine law.

No man, therefore, who is not Bishop of Rome can be successor of St. Peter either in that See or in the primacy over the whole Church, which was by the disposition of the divine providence bound up therewith, as is attested by the fact that whatever differences may have existed among men as to the divine institution of the primacy, possession of the primacy has never either been claimed by, or attributed to, any man who did not at the same time claim to be the one rightful Bishop of the Roman Church.

He who is lawfully elected to the Roman Bishopric receives the power of primacy immediately from God. He does not receive it from the Church, nor from his electors to the Bishopric. The Church cannot give that which it does not itself possess. The primacy is over the Church, and that by divine law. As the Church of Christ is subject to Christ, so is it also subject to the Vicar of Christ, for otherwise he would not be Christ's Vicar in his relation to Christ's Church, and Christ would be subject to His Church in the person of His Vicar.

The predecessor of a Pontiff has power to constitute the form of election to the Roman Bishopric, and so to determine the way in which his successor is to be elected to that Bishopric; but once elected to the Bishopric of Rome the elect receives, and that immediately from Christ Himself, the power of primacy. It is obtained not from man, but in virtue of the divine law of the institution of the primacy in Peter,—the perpetuity of a series of successors to Peter in the primacy,—and the mode of succession through possession of the Roman See, with which the primacy is divinely bound up.

The functions of the electors, whoever they may

be—the Cardinals, as at present, or others, as in times past—is to designate the person who is to occupy the vacant See of Rome. The mode of designation has not been determined by God by any divine law, and so it remains free to be determined by ecclesiastical law. But, given lawful election, that is, election in accordance with laws laid down by preceding Pontiffs, the Bishop-Elect is by divine law Vicar of Christ, from whom immediately he receives the primacy.

Supreme and universal jurisdiction over the whole Church and over all and every one of the faithful is therefore possessed by the Roman Bishop-Elect as soon as he is elected, and before he is consecrated Bishop. The power of episcopal order, which is conferred by episcopal consecration, does not in any case carry with it episcopal jurisdiction. That is received by Bishops-Elect from the Roman Pontiff, when their election is confirmed by him. But there is no power in the Church on earth which is higher than that of the Vicar of Christ, and so there is no power on earth from whom he, when elected Bishop, can receive confirmation; and since he is the one source of jurisdiction in the visible Church, there is no source upon earth from which he can receive it. He receives it from Him alone of whom he is the Vicar.

The primacy of the Vicar of Christ, being always one and the self-same primacy, the power of the Roman Pontiff remains always the same. It cannot be diminished by acts of predecessors, nor can any Pontiff diminish his own power. The Vicar of Christ is not Christ, but only Christ's Vicar, and it is not in his power to lessen that which Christ has Himself established.

THE
VICAR OF CHRIST.

II.

HIS RELATION TO THE CHURCH OF CHRIST.

On that occasion when Jesus selected one man, and made him to be His Vicar upon the earth, He spoke to that man of the Church which He intended to build.

This Church was to endure to the end of time, and throughout all time there was to exist upon the earth not only a Church of Christ, but a Vicar of Christ.

Jesus had created His Vicar before He built His Church. The creation of His Vicar was on that day at Cæsarea Philippi an act of the then present—the building of His Church was on that day only a purpose of His to be carried out in the future. He said, "*I will build* My Church," but He had already said to Simon of Bethsaida, "*Thou art* Peter" (the Rock). He had laid the foundation before He reared upon it the superstructure.

An architect who has planned, and who intends to build a house, may select a rock on which, as on a firm foundation, he means to build it. Some time may however elapse before he builds the house, and during that time the chosen rock is not as yet a foundation. It is nevertheless the chosen site on which the house is to be built. When the house is actually built, it becomes the foundation of that which is raised upon it. That which it then becomes it can never cease to be, so long as the house continues to exist.

Jesus, in making Simon to be the Rock, made him to be His Vicar, inasmuch as He is Himself the *principal* Rock. In making Simon to be Peter, He made him to be, by communication and participation, that which He Himself was and is, as He is the Rock.

Jesus might have willed to leave upon the earth a visible Vicar, without leaving upon the earth a visible Church.

But such was not His will, and this He declared when He said, " I will build My Church." He declared His further will that there should be an indissoluble bond between that Church and Peter, when, having already said to Simon, " Thou art Peter" (the Rock), He added, " And upon this Rock I will build My Church." He thus established between that Church and Peter the same necessary relation as that which exists and must exist between a house and the foundation on which it is built.

Jesus might have made Peter to be His Vicar for only a certain time, and this Peter might have been if he had been made to be merely the Vicar of Christ. But when Jesus connected Peter with His Church, which was to endure throughout all time—and connected it with him as inseparably as a superstructure is connected with its foundation—He guaranteed the permanence of His Vicar in his relation to His Church. The perpetuity of a visible Vicar of Christ was thus bound up with the perpetuity of the visible Church of Christ.

This visible Church of Christ is a society of mortal men who are still living upon the earth. It is a society moreover which was constituted *by Christ Himself.* He said not, "On this Rock shall be built," He said, "On this Rock *I will build My Church.*"

In every society of men there must be one central authority, the action of which extends to every one of the members who compose that society. This authority is to a society that which a foundation is to the house that is built upon it. It is the basis of its stability and of its unity. So long as the members of a society remain subject to its central authority, the society continues to exist, and its members form one society. No one who is not subject to this central authority is or can be a member of that society. He is outside its pale, and has no share in its rights, or privileges, or endowments. It is as necessary in a society for its members to be subject to its central authority, as it is necessary for the walls of a house to lie upon the lines of its foundation. Any buildings erected outside those lines form no part of that house.

The central authority which, by its exercise of power, binds the members of a society together, must be as external and visible as is the society itself. Mere agreement between the members, or internal union of minds and wills, will not secure the stability of a society, and will not constitute a society as such—that is, it will not make an assembly of men to be a society, properly so called.

The authority which constitutes a society may be determined by the society itself, or rather by the men who, desiring to found a society, determine that central authority which shall constitute it, and to which they submit themselves, and so become members of the society thus created.

If Jesus, when He departed from this earth,

had left behind Him individual disciples only, and these had met together with the intention and desire of founding a society for the dissemination of His doctrine, and had chosen a head, and had invested this head with that authority which is sufficient to bind men together as members in one body, there would have existed upon the earth a society of men for the dissemination of the doctrine of Christ—but that society would not have been formed *by Christ*, and it would not have been that Church which Jesus said *He was to build.* It would have been a merely human association for religious purposes.

Further, if Jesus had not carried out His intention before He left the earth of building His Church, and had left only His Vicar upon the earth to represent Him, and that Vicar had founded a Church, that Church would have been in a sense a divine society, inasmuch as it was founded by divine authority—but it would not have been a Church *built by Jesus Christ Himself* in person. Jesus would have laid the foundation, but He would not have been Himself the Builder. His words, "*I will build* My Church," would not have been verified by it. The same authority that had built that Church could have altered or modified its constitution. What the Vicar of Christ had done, the Vicar of Christ could undo.

But when Jesus *Himself built His own* Church, what He did His Vicar has no power to undo. Whatsoever in that Church was instituted and constituted by Jesus Christ must remain ever intact, even as He left it. He made His Vicar to be the perpetual foundation of His Church, and the supreme authority within it, but *He Himself built* His Church, and laid it on that foundation, and His Vicar has no power to alter that divine structure. He has no power, for instance, to abolish the government of the Church by means of Bishops, or to add to the number of the sacraments, since these are of divine institution, and are of the essence of the Church *as Christ built it.*

Herein is manifest the difference between that which is of *divine* law, and that which is of *ecclesiastical* law. The Vicar of Christ is the source of ecclesiastical law, and the laws which he has made he can unmake. Whatsoever he has power to bind on men, he has power to loose men from, as well as to bind it again upon them—but with that which is of divine law he cannot interfere. He has not made it, and he cannot unmake it. He has power indeed to interpret it as he is supreme judge, but he has no power to deal with it as if he had been its legislator. He is the true Vicar of Christ, but he is His Vicar only, and he is not the Christ.

The Church of Christ is called in the inspired Scriptures the Body of Christ. The men upon earth who compose the visible Church are members of that Body, and of it Christ is Himself the Head. So long as Christ was on earth, dwelling visibly in the midst of His visible members, He was Himself their visible Head. When He departed from this earth, he whom He had made to be His Vicar was left *in His place* as visible Head of the visible Church.

Christ, although He is not visibly present upon earth, is nevertheless visible in Himself in virtue of His risen Body, and He remains the Supreme Head of His visible Church. It does not, however, follow that that Church has two heads. Christ and His Vicar together constitute one Head, inasmuch as the authority that exists in both is one and the same authority. The one authority is that of Christ, which he exercises by means of His Vicar. It is not as if His Vicar possessed all the authority of Christ, for, as we have seen, there are certain things which Christ has done, and which His Vicar cannot do. But all the authority which Christ's Vicar does possess and exercise is the authority of Christ. In Christ it is *original*, while in His Vicar it is *derived*.

If there were no visible Head of the Church on earth, the external action of Christ, as He is the Head, could not be exercised and brought home to the members of His Body. With these He is in immediate contact through His Vicar. He personates Christ, and thus they are brought under the influence of Christ's action. A king who had travelled into a country far distant from his kingdom could not exercise his royal authority, and make it felt by his subjects, unless he had left behind him a viceroy in his place, to whom they should be subject, and whom they should be bound to obey. But the existence of the viceroy does not result in there being two kings of one kingdom, since all the authority of the viceroy is the authority of the king, which through and by means of him reaches to the subjects of the king.

Thus did Jesus provide for the unity of the Church which He built. He secured it by means of the connection which He established between His visible Church and His visible Vicar upon the earth—the connection between a house and the rock which is its foundation.

The primacy of the Vicar of Christ was instituted not merely to *preserve* the visible Church in its unity, but to *effect* that unity. It was not merely to keep the Church one, but to make it to be one.

Apart from this primacy there could not be the unity which exists in, and is characteristic of, that Church which Christ Himself built. The Church of Christ is one, because the Vicar of Christ is one. It is his oneness which gives to the Church its oneness, and he was put in his place by Christ before the Church was built by Christ.

The unity of particular or local Churches, as they are parts of that homogeneous whole which is the Universal Church, is also effected through the primacy of the Vicar of Christ. They are not to be conceived as if they were separate Churches, each with its own independent unity, and all banded together under one president. The Church which Christ built was not a confederation of separate Churches. It was one Church—one and the same in every land—one house on one foundation—one kingdom under one sovereign—one flock under one pastor—one visible Body with one visible Head. The Church of Christ is thus one, as Christ is one, and this it could not be if there were no Vicar of Christ upon the earth.

2

It follows from the primacy of the Roman Pontiff, as he is the Vicar of Christ, that his jurisdiction is *ordinary* and *immediate* over all and every one of the faithful.

Ordinary jurisdiction is a technical term, and by it is meant that authority over subjects which is attached to an office or dignity *by law*,—in contradistinction to the authority which is possessed by delegation from some superior, and which is called *extraordinary* jurisdiction. He possesses *ordinary* jurisdiction who is established in the office or dignity to which jurisdiction is *by law* attached, and from which that jurisdiction cannot be separated. He does not require jurisdiction to be bestowed upon him after his appointment to his office. It is conveyed in that office with which it is inseparably bound up.

The jurisdiction of the Vicar of Christ must necessarily be *ordinary* jurisdiction, or that jurisdiction which of right and by law belongs to the office and dignity of him who is Vicar of Christ. It cannot possibly be delegated to him by any superior, inasmuch as the Vicar of Christ cannot possibly have any superior upon earth. It cannot be delegated to him by the Universal Church, for that Church is subject unto Christ, and by such delegation Christ would, in the person of His Vicar, be made subject to His own Church. Christ has Himself attached supremacy of jurisdiction to the office of His Vicar, and so he who is placed in that office is, in virtue of divine law, invested with that jurisdiction, and receives it immediately from Him whose Vicar he is.

Mediate jurisdiction is also a technical term, and by it is meant that authority which is exercised over superiors of subjects, and which reaches those subjects only through their immediate superiors. *Immediate* jurisdiction is that which is exercised as over one's own proper subjects, and without any necessity for the intervention of any intermediate authority.

In the actual exercise of immediate jurisdiction, there may indeed be interposition of subordinate superiors, and this there must be when the subjects are many in number, as in the case of a kingdom. It would be physically impossible for any king to bring his royal authority to bear on every one of his subjects directly and individually. He therefore exercises it by means of subordinate officials. These are along with the king the immediate superiors of those whom he has made subject to them. The king nevertheless retains his power to deal directly with any one of those subjects, and therefore he remains the *immediate* superior of all his subjects.

The ordinary jurisdiction of the Roman Pontiff —and that it is *ordinary* no one can deny who does not deny the primacy—is *immediate* over all and every one of the faithful. The primacy was instituted by Christ in order that the jurisdiction of His Vicar should be thus immediate.

Those therefore would be in error who should

hold that the Vicar of Christ is the Head of the Church of Christ, simply because he is first among the members of the ecclesiastical hierarchy. They would also be in error who should maintain that the position which he holds with regard to the whole Church is only through the intermediate hierarchy, or that he is Universal Bishop of the Universal Church in the sense only that he is Bishop of Bishops. He is Bishop of Bishops, indeed, but he is the *immediate* Bishop also of every one of the faithful of the flock of Christ.

The Vicar of Christ alone has from Christ the keys of the Kingdom. He has power to bind and to loose all persons whomsoever, and all things whatsoever in the Church, as he may see fit. No one can loose what Christ's Vicar binds, and no one can bind what he looses. In his exercise of his supreme and universal immediate jurisdiction, he is independent of every one, and he has no need of the concurrence of any one.

Every pastor, as such, must have some sheep committed to him to feed with immediate jurisdiction, but to His Vicar Christ gave not some of His sheep, but all of His sheep—all the faithful, priests and people, Bishops and Apostles—when He said to Peter, " Feed My lambs ; feed My sheep," for besides the sheep that are Christ's there are no others in the Church of Christ.

The jurisdiction of the Vicar of Christ extends immediately to all and to every one of the Bishops. They are, as it were, the columns of the Church which Christ built upon the Rock, and on that Rock they have been laid by Him. The Bishops are true princes in Christ's Kingdom, but as princes they are subject to Christ the King in the person of His Vicar. They are as the sheep in the flock of Christ, to whom the lambs are subject, but they with these are themselves subject to the Vicar of the one Supreme Pastor. In comparison with their priests and people the Bishops are as pastors—in comparison with Christ's Vicar they are themselves but as sheep of the fold. Hence the Roman Pontiff is called the Bishop of Bishops, the Pastor of Pastors, the Father of Fathers, as well as the Universal Bishop, or Bishop of the Universal Church.

That to which the Rock has its relation is the whole Church which was built by Christ upon it. That to which the Viceroy, in whose hands have been placed the keys of the Kingdom, has his relation is the whole Kingdom of the King. That to which the Supreme Pastor has his relation is the whole flock of Christ. The Vicar of Christ rules all, not inasmuch as he rules every one, but on the contrary he rules every one inasmuch as he rules all. His immediate power falls first on the Church—the Kingdom—the Flock, and then on the individual members, the subjects and sheep. These he immediately rules, inasmuch as they belong to the Kingdom and Flock, which is the Universal Church.

The Vicar of Christ has not only supreme *executive* power, he has also supreme *legislative* and *judicial* power. These powers belong to him independently of the consent and will of the Church.

Such power is truly episcopal, for episcopal power is ordinary and immediate power of jurisdiction. It is that authority over subjects, which in its completeness is at once legislative, judicial, and executive. The Pontiff's power is not only truly episcopal, but it is episcopal power in its utmost excellence. Not only can nothing be lawfully done in the Church against his will, but every other power in the Church is directly dependent on his will.

The power of the Vicar of Christ either formally or virtually embraces every other power in the Church of Christ. It is therefore the immediate fountain from which flows the jurisdiction of every one of the Bishops.

This is demanded by the very nature of the primacy, as it was instituted by Christ Himself. He who so holds the keys that he opens and no man can shut, and shuts and no man can open, has power of such a nature that no one can open or shut, without his at the same time opening and shutting, or giving power to open or to shut. If any one had power without him, or apart from power bestowed by him, to open or to shut, it might so happen that while he was opening, another should be shutting, or that while he was shutting another should be opening. Apart therefore from the supreme and immediate authority of the Vicar of Christ, there cannot be exercise of any power in the Church of Christ.

The Bishops, although their jurisdiction, or authority over subjects, is immediately dependent on the Pontiff, are nevertheless not the delegates or the vicars of the Vicar of Christ. They are equally with him of divine institution. By the institution of Christ Himself they are ordinary pastors of particular flocks within the one fold of the Universal Church. They are true territorial princes within the one world-wide Kingdom. They are, however, at the same time immediately dependent on Christ's Vicar, inasmuch as they receive jurisdiction from him who alone received the keys of the Kingdom. He can validly take away the jurisdiction of any Bishop, and that apart from any certain cause, and without assigning any reason. Were it otherwise, his jurisdiction would not be supreme, and a limit would be placed to the words of Christ—" *Whatsoever* thou shalt bind on earth shall be bound in Heaven, and whatsoever thou shalt loose on earth shall be loosed in Heaven "—which has not been placed by the action of Christ Himself.

That only is excluded from the universal jurisdiction of Christ's Vicar—conveyed by the universal words of Christ, taken in their connection with His preceding words to Peter, "To thee will I give the keys of the Kingdom of Heaven"—which has been of the nature of the case excluded by some other institution of His, such as is His institution of Bishops. But His institution of Bishops in His Church is in no way incompatible with His will that the jurisdiction which they receive and exercise should be in entire dependence on His Vicar.

Christ's institution of vicarious power, on the other hand, demands that all the jurisdiction which He exercises in His Church, He should exercise through his Vicar—and to confer jurisdiction is itself an act of jurisdiction.

While the Vicar of Christ can validly withdraw the jurisdiction of any Bishop—a power which is necessarily included in his supremacy of jurisdiction—it is not in his power to abolish episcopal jurisdiction. He has no power to govern the Church without Bishops who are furnished with true episcopal jurisdiction—a jurisdiction which is legislative, judicial, and executive over those portions of the flock which are entrusted to their individual pastoral care. This is the jurisdiction which is proper to a Bishop. While complete within its own sphere, it remains, however, always subordinate to that supreme and universal jurisdiction by which the Universal Church is governed. Individual Bishops cannot therefore do anything contrary to the Common Law which extends to and binds the Universal Church. They cannot do anything in matters which of themselves affect the Universal Church, and generally, they cannot deal with what are called " greater causes," for these the Universal Bishop has reserved for his own decision. It is not for Bishops to determine what are the limits of their episcopal power. In all cases of controversy, with regard to those limits, the supreme judge, from whom there can be no appeal, is the one Vicar of Christ.

It is to him, as the nature of the primacy demands, that it belongs to judge the judgments of the Bishops, and either to rescind or to confirm them. He from whose final judgment there can be no appeal has the right to receive appeals from all and every one of his subjects—not only from a Bishop, as against the judgment of a Synod of Bishops, but from any priest or layman against the judgment of his Bishop. The power of Christ's Vicar is *immediate*, and therefore he has the right to investigate and judge all the causes of all and every one of the faithful. His power is *supreme*, and therefore it is his right that no sentence with regard to any one of the faithful should be peremptory apart from his consent, since every one of them is his own immediate subject. Superiors of their subjects are themselves his immediate subjects, and an ultimately peremptory, or final sentence without appeal, cannot be given save by supreme authority alone.

This, as an inherent right of the primacy, is a right divinely bestowed. It is not derived from any human or ecclesiastical law, but is directly derived from divine law. The Pontiff may himself will that it should not be lawful for his subjects to appeal to him in all causes, and he may by his own will permit appeals only in certain causes, if this should seem to him to be for the general good of the Church at large. But in thus restricting appeals to himself, he would be in reality exercising his own right, and in no way renouncing a right which Christ has given to His Vicar, and of which no lesser power can deprive him.

3

It belongs to Jesus Christ, not only to rule and govern, but to *teach* mankind. He has therefore not only given to His Vicar upon earth the keys of the Kingdom, but He has established him in His visible Church as the Confirmer of his brethren in their faith. His faith, as he is their Confirmer, must be unfailing,—it must be impossible for him to err in doctrine,—he must necessarily be infallible in his teaching with regard to all matters of faith and morals.

Christ came to teach men that which their Maker would have them to believe and do. That which He taught they could not know with absolute certainty, unless it came to them with infallible authority. This authority belongs to that Church which Jesus built, and it belongs as in its source to His Vicar, on whom, as on a Rock, He founded His Church. The Vicar of Christ is the efficacious principle of the infallibility of the Church of Christ.

Christ instituted Bishops in His Church, and placing them as pastors of particular flocks within the one Fold, He willed that they should be authoritative witnesses and teachers, who should preach and preserve and propagate throughout all time the truths of His Divine Revelation. As in their ruling, so also in their teaching, He made them subordinate to one Universal Teacher, whose faith should be unfailing, and who should confirm them as his brethren in their faith and teaching. No one or other or all together of those subordinate teachers did He make to be in themselves infallible.

The Universal Church which Christ built possesses the infallibility of Christ, but in that Church is included the Vicar of Christ, and it is from him, as from its source, that the infallibility of the Church flows. Apart from him it would not be the Church of Christ, and it would be severed from the wellspring of infallibility.

The infallibility of the Church of Christ and of the Vicar of Christ—who are bound up together in one by Christ, as is a house with the rock which is its foundation—is effected through the assistance and direction of the Holy Ghost. He descended on the Day of Pentecost on Peter and the Apostles—on the living Rock, and on those living columns which were laid thereon—to abide throughout all time in that Church which Christ built, and to guide those who dwell therein unto all the truth.

To the Vicar of Christ the Holy Ghost does not *reveal*, neither does He *inspire* him as He inspired the Sacred Writers. The Holy Ghost so *directs* Christ's Vicar's mind that it apprehends as true that which is really true, and so directs his will that he teaches as to be believed by all the faithful that which has been either explicitly revealed, or is implicitly and therefore necessarily contained in the Divine Revelation.

The Vicar of Christ is then certainly infallible when he teaches the Church of Christ as he is the Vicar of Christ—that is, when he exercises his office of Pastor and Teacher of all the faithful,

THE VICAR OF CHRIST.

and with his supreme Apostolic authority defines doctrine concerning faith or morals, as to be held by the Universal Church.

He is then said to speak *ex Cathedrâ*, from the Chair—the Chair of Peter—his Chair, as he is Vicar of Christ. Such utterances from that Chair are infallible in themselves, and not from any preceding, or concomitant, or subsequent consent of the Church. His teaching cannot derive its infallibility from her the infallibility of whose teaching is derived from his.

It is one thing to believe, and to profess belief in a truth, and it is another thing to be the teacher of that truth. The whole body of the faithful may hold a doctrine which is divinely true, and yet that body is not the teacher of the doctrine. The whole body of the Bishops may be a teacher of truth, and may nevertheless be an infallible teacher only as it is in union with, in subordination to, and confirmed by the supreme teaching authority of the Vicar of Christ, whom Christ has made to be the Rock of the faith and the Confirmer of his brethren therein.

Universal teaching authority is an authority which demands belief from the Universal Church. It involves jurisdiction over the whole Church. So to teach is an act of supreme authority, and that resides neither in the body of the faithful, nor in the body of the Bishops, but in him alone who is the visible Head of both. In his person infallibility of teaching and supreme power of jurisdiction have been bound up together by Christ. It can never, therefore, suggest itself to men that looking to the one they are bound to believe, while, looking to the other, they are free from all obligation.

The Vicar of Christ is the one and only *immediate subject* of infallibility, that is, he alone is by himself, and not through or by means of another, infallible. The Church of Christ is infallible, but only along with and through the Vicar of Christ, when he teaches, or confirms the teaching of its pastors.

It belongs to the Vicar of Christ, and to him alone as of right, to call together the pastors of the Church of Christ in Council. The Bishops assembled by his convocation in Council differ from the same Bishops as dispersed throughout the world, and each in his own diocese. There each has power over only that particular diocese. Each operates apart, and independently of the other Bishops. In a Council all contribute their operations, counsels, and suffrages, so that of the acts of all there is constituted one act.

In a Council the Bishops exercise their episcopal power, not only over their own dioceses, but over the province of dioceses to which they belong, if the Council is Provincial: and over the Universal Church, if the Council is Œcumenical.

Convocation of Councils may be understood in various ways, either as it is an act of jurisdiction over those who are called, which lays upon them the obligation to attend—or as it is merely an act of ministry, done by way of service and in support of the jurisdiction of him who alone has power to convoke a Council—or by way of counsel and exhortation, as when the Bishops beg the Pontiff to call a Council for the promotion of the welfare of the Church. This they can do, but it is not in their power, apart from him, to convoke a Council.

An Œcumenical Council is therefore impossible during a vacancy of the Apostolic See. The Bishops can indeed assemble, as in cases of hindrance to the election of a Pontiff, or at times the circumstances of which would render the election of a lawful Pontiff doubtful, apart from such an assembly. This they have the right to do, and this they ought to do for the welfare of the Christian commonwealth. But in such cases they have power only to take steps to secure the election of a Pontiff, to the lawfulness of whose election no doubt can attach. They have no power to make laws for the Universal Church. This they cannot do apart from the universal authority of a Vicar of Christ. They may, by way of preparation, draw up some schemes of law, but these have no force of obligation, until there is a Pontiff, and he has confirmed them.

If the whole body of the Bishops has not the power to convoke an Œcumenical Council, still less can it be supposed for a moment that any civil ruler has or can have this power. When we read of Emperors calling Councils of the Church, we are to understand that they did so by way of ministerial convocation only. It was done in fulfilment of a duty, and not as an exercise of a right. It is the duty of Christian Emperors, and of other civil rulers, to use the power at their disposal in aid and support and defence of the Church of Christ. When they have at times of their own accord done this service, and the Vicar of Christ has recognized it as being for the benefit of the Church, he has by permitting it, lent to their spontaneous action the sanction of his supreme authority. There was, moreover, a time when a law of the Empire forbade the holding of public assemblies without the consent of the Emperor. This law was for the general good, and the Vicar of Christ recognized this when he asked the consent of the Emperor for the convocation of a Council of the Church. His consent was also practically necessary, not by way of right, but by way of co-operation, at a time when vehicles of transit were not at the service of the public generally, but at the disposal of the Emperor, whose leave had to be obtained for the use of them. The expense also of bringing so many Bishops from far distant countries, and of supporting them during the continuance of a Council, was so great that it could not have been defrayed otherwise than from the Imperial treasury. A Council, although convoked by the Pontiff, would, apart from the co-operation of the Emperor, have been at some times a physical impossibility.

Whatever individual Emperors may have intended, or whatever the prudent condescension of the Roman Pontiffs may have been with regard to the

Emperors in the matter, the principle remains certain that the Pontiff alone has the right and power of jurisdiction so to convoke a Council as to lay the Bishops under a religious obligation to attend it. That neither the Bishops themselves, nor any civil rulers possess this power of convocation which belongs to supreme authority, cannot be denied without perversion of the economy of the Church, as instituted by Christ, and introduction of either aristocratic or popular rule, or enslaving the Church to the civil power.

A second right which belongs to the Vicar of Christ with regard to Councils of the Church of Christ is his right to *preside*. This is not a mere matter of honour. It is a right which follows from the very nature of the primacy as instituted by Christ, and its accompanying prerogative of infallibility, which belongs to jurisdiction. The Roman Pontiffs have always presided at Œcumenical Councils, either in person, or through their Legates.

With the rights of convoking and of presiding

in Councils, there is bound up the right to propose or determine the matter for deliberation and judgment. The Pontiff can always exclude any matter whatsoever from discussion, since he has simply to withhold the power of jurisdiction which is necessary for an act of judgment with regard to it.

Even if the jurisdiction of the Bishops over their own dioceses were immediately from Christ, and not immediately from the Vicar of Christ, their jurisdiction in a Council would be immediately from Christ's Vicar. The act of making laws which are to bind the Universal Church, is an act which of necessity requires supreme authority. This they can derive from him alone, without whose consent no obligation can be laid upon the whole Church of Christ.

Bishops in a Council are judges of faith. They are not mere consultors. An exercise of their power of judgment is required, not for a judgment, but for a *Conciliar* judgment. There will not have been a judgment *of the Council*, unless the whole or the greater part of the Bishops have given consent thereto. The Vicar of Christ can by himself alone define, but he cannot make his definition to be a *Conciliar* definition. There cannot be a conciliar definition without *the Sacred Council approving.*

The Bishops in a Council have the right to *examine* even that which the Vicar of Christ has already defined. Their examination does not spring from doubt with regard to the truth of that which he has defined. They have, on the contrary, absolute certainty with regard to it, by reason of his infallibility in defining. In order to certainty there must be a motive which is sufficient to beget it, and here it is—infallible authority. But that motive does not exclude other motives. Since there may remain some doubt with regard to the existence or character of these, this doubt renders examination possible. The Bishops already know that the doctrine which has been defined is true, but they may not as yet know the testimonies of Scripture or Tradition on which it also rests—or the reasonings from the analogy of the faith by which it may be illustrated—or the arguments by which it may be best defended from the cavils of heretics.

This examination is most important for the sake of the Bishops themselves, as they are authoritative teachers of the faith in their own dioceses. They have to teach to their own subjects the doctrine which the Vicar of Christ has defined, and they ought to know in what way it may be best set before their subjects in all its fulness, and at all points defended against the adversaries of the faith.

For this reason not only is a Pontifical definition submitted to the examination of the Bishops in a Council, but a Conciliar definition may be in like manner recalled to examination in a subsequent Council. This cannot possibly be for the revocation or reformation of that definition, since that which is infallible is irreformable. It is in order that greater light may be thrown upon the truth defined—that it may be more fully unfolded—or that it may be made more impregnable to its assailants. Thus we find that that which was solemnly defined in the Second Council of Lyons, with regard to the procession of the Holy Ghost from the Father and the Son, and with regard to the supreme and plenary primacy of the Roman Church over the Universal Church, was in both instances recalled to examination in the Council of Florence. The doctrine of Transubstantiation was defined in the Fourth Lateran Council, and it was recalled to examination in the Council of Trent, for assertion as against the Protestants.

After this examination there comes the *Suffrage*, by which the doctrine is approved.

The Bishops have by this time sufficient knowledge of the cause, and, inasmuch as they are judges, they are bound to give judgment. A judge who is called on by his superior to give judgment, and who is then actually sitting as a judge, is bound, after there has been due discussion of the cause, to execute his office, and do his duty by giving his judgment. He is not free to judge or not to judge. He is there for the very purpose of giving judgment, and he is bound to do so, as well as to judge in accordance with that which he knows to be the truth.

When the Bishops in a Council give their suffrages along with the Vicar of Christ, they then one and all truly define, and that with their own authority. They possess divine authority, in virtue of their institution by Christ to be pastors of His flock, to teach the faithful, and to judge in causes of faith. Of this authority definition is an act.

Their definition, by itself and apart from the definition of the Vicar of Christ, is imperfect indeed and incomplete, in the same way as their authority to teach is incomplete in itself, and apart from the supreme authority of Christ's Vicar. Their definition is nevertheless an authoritative definition, just as a judgment which may be appealed from is really a judicial judgment, although it is not a final judgment. That judgment perseveres until it is reversed. If it is sustained on appeal, that which is then carried out is not the judgment of the court of appeal, but the judgment of the judge which that court has affirmed.

When therefore the Bishops along with Christ's Vicar teach, they are assumed to a share of his supreme authority to teach the Universal Church. Of their judicial acts along with his, there is constituted one act of conciliar definition, and it is final.

His definition, apart from theirs, would be final, but not conciliar—their definition, apart from his, would be neither final nor conciliar—their definition, along with his, is both final and conciliar. They along with him do truly finally define, inasmuch as they are truly along with him the cause of that one act of all concerned, which is a conciliar definition, and is final.

The character of this judgment which is given by the Bishops in a Council will appear more clearly if it is contrasted with the judgments of theologians, or of others who are not Bishops. These are not of the number of the pastors who were instituted by Jesus Christ Himself to feed His flock. They do not therefore judge with the pastoral authority which these possess, and the faithful are not their subjects. Even if the Vicar of Christ should associate them with himself in his judgment, he alone would then be judging, and they would not be judging along with him, as do the Bishops in a Council.

There is no essential difference between a definition made solely by the Vicar of Christ, and a conciliar definition. The value of both is essentially the same. The authority of the Bishops cannot add force to that which has already supreme authority. Their definition cannot confirm that by which it is itself confirmed. But a conciliar definition, as it is the visible act of the whole body of the visible Church of Christ, along with its visible Head, the Vicar of Christ, is externally a more striking and splendid manifestation of revealed truth as divinely taught, and of the unity in faith of that teaching authority which Jesus Christ has established upon earth.

To say that there may be appeal from the Vicar of Christ to a Council, is *schismatical*, since it denies the subjection, in organic and vital union, of the visible Church to its visible Head. It is also *heretical*, as directly subversive of the doctrine of the primacy over the whole Church which Christ has instituted in His Vicar, whom He made to be the living Rock on which His Church is built, the one Keeper of the keys of His Kingdom, the Confirmer of his brethren in their faith, and the Supreme Pastor of all the faithful. It is moreover *absurd*, inasmuch as the assembly appealed to will either comprehend the Vicar of Christ, or not. If not, it will not be a Council of the Church of Christ. If it comprehends Christ's Vicar, appeal is incomprehensible from him to that which can have existence only by his will—to that in which he has plenary and supreme authority—and any decree of which he can by his simple negative annul.

5

The visible Church of Christ is the Kingdom of Christ upon the earth. Its government is monarchical, and this not by the will of the Church, but by the will of Him who built His Church on that one man whom He had made to be the living Rock, which was to serve as its foundation, and to whom He gave the keys of His Kingdom. That man Jesus made to be His Vicar both in teaching and in ruling. In ruling, he is Viceroy of the King.

In the Universal Church we find all the elements of monarchy in its purest form. One Sovereign rules the whole commonwealth—he has plenitude of power—all other magisterial authorities are subordinate and subject to him—he can judge every one of them, and no one of them has power to judge him—and to him, as he is the efficacious principle and centre of the unity of the whole society, all who will to remain members of that society, and to share in its privileges, must submit themselves.

Democratic government would be subversive of the very idea of the Universal Church, as it is the Kingdom of Christ. He certainly did not institute His Church as a democracy, in which the supreme power springs from, and is exercised by the society itself. As certainly He did not institute His Church as an oligarchy, for equal power was not given by Him to all His Apostles. They were placed by Him under one Pastor and Prince, who had a primacy of jurisdiction even over them. It is true that Christ tempered the monarchical constitution of His Church with an aristocratic element, by His institution of Bishops, as these are true princes in His Kingdom; but that is in no way incompatible with the monarchy which He instituted, inasmuch as the Bishops are not the equals of Christ's Vicar in jurisdiction, nor does their jurisdiction hinder the plenitude of his power.

The monarchical constitution of the Universal Church is manifest even during a vacancy of the

Viceroy's Chair. Supreme power of ruling does not then exist in the whole body of the Church, as in a democracy. Neither does it exist in the Bishops collectively, as in an aristocracy. The actual exercise of it is impossible until there exists one man to whom, by the divine law of the institution of Christ, the primacy shall belong, and who shall receive neither from the Church, nor from the Bishops, but directly and immediately from Jesus Christ Himself, that supremacy of jurisdiction in virtue of which he shall be His Vicar and Viceroy.

Until there is thus again a Vicar of Christ upon the earth, no doctrine can be defined—nor can any law, properly so called, be made,—and no law of any previous Vicar can be abrogated.

The Church is not, however, during that time destitute of all authority for its government. The power of the Bishops continues as it was before. This power had flowed to them, indeed, from him who had been Vicar of Christ, but it does not cease to exist when he has passed away. Their power, as ordinary, is attached to their office, and with that office it endures. It does not, however, now rise above its level. It remains as incomplete a power as it was before, apart from the supreme authority of a Vicar of Christ. The Church remains as much bound as it was before by the divine law of the primacy as instituted by Christ. There remains also as much necessity as ever for the embodiment and actual exercise of supreme authority. The Bishops continue to conduct themselves as they conducted themselves during the lifetime of Christ's Vicar. They continue to exercise that authority which they received from him. They do not vindicate for themselves, individually or collectively, supreme authority, and they recognize the necessity of a visible Head in a Vicar of Christ.

The Vicar's Chair is said therefore to remain, even while it is vacant of an occupant, in the sense that that Chair is the vicarious authority which is perpetual by the law of its institution, and which is therefore one and the self-same authority in all who exercise it. While the Chair is vacant, there can be no actual exercise of the supreme authority which it represents, but that authority remains in effect in the continued exercise of the subordinate authority which was derived therefrom.

Thus is the monarchy of Christ maintained in His Kingdom on the earth, and at no time is its perpetuity more manifest than it is when for a time it seems to be in abeyance. There is no other way in which the royalty of Christ could be made a reality to men, than that way in which He has chosen to press it home upon them. Without a visible Viceroy the King might reign indeed from His Throne in Heaven, but He would in no real sense bear rule over His subjects on the earth. In His Vicar Christ's subjects recognize their Sovereign, and do him homage, and then more than ever do they *feel* the necessity of a Viceroy's presence in their midst, when for a time his throne is vacant.

THE VICAR OF CHRIST

III.

HIS RELATION TO CIVIL SOCIETY.

CIVIL society is the creation of God. Man is of his nature a social being. He finds himself, at his entrance into the world, a member of a human society. In that society he is a subject, and he has superiors. A man's parents are his superiors in that primary society which is called the family.

The head of the woman is the man, and God has made wives to be subject to their husbands. To both husband and wife are their children subject by the ordinance of God.

Every family is a true society, inasmuch as it contains a principle of authority, which is the centre of its unity. Apart from authority a society cannot exist. Without unity there cannot be one individual society. A society consists of superior and subjects, and it is the authority of the superior which constitutes it, or makes it to be a society.

A society which is a unity in itself may form part of an aggregate of societies, which together form one society. This larger society is, like the individual societies of which it consists, constituted a society by the presence within it of a principle of authority, which is the centre of its unity. There must be one superior of the larger society, to whom the superiors as well as the subjects of the included societies are subject.

Human families are following the social tendency in human nature, when they associate themselves in societies of which they then form parts. The existence of a social ruler is a necessary consequence of every such association, if it is to be a true society.

A society of families is a *civil* society—or society of fellow-citizens—and these are subject to a superior. who is their *civil* ruler.

The family does not lose its individuality in the civil society of which it forms part, nor is the authority of the domestic superior lost in that of the civil ruler. The father retains his rights within his family, and it is only an abuse of those rights which would bring his exercise of them under the restraint of the civil ruler. The domestic power is antecedent to the civil power, and its roots lie deeper in human nature.

In the domestic society there can be no question as to who the domestic ruler is to be. In a civil society the question with regard to the civil ruler is not so determined by the nature of the case.

In civil society there is no precise form of civil government which is of directly divine determination. But the *form* of government is distinct from the *power* with which the civil ruler governs. Whatever the form of government may be, that power is from God. There exists by ordinance of God, a power in civil society which is a participation of the divine power. He who is the one source of all being must necessarily be the one source of all power, and of every power which exists in any being. Apart from participation of the divine power, there cannot be lawful power in any man over his fellow-men.

It follows that, since civil power is from God, it cannot be exercised as if it were independent of God—civil society cannot reasonably be Godless—and a civil ruler cannot have the right to rule as if there were no God.

The immediate end of the civil ruler is the *temporal* welfare of his subjects in the civil society which he governs. But the temporal welfare of immortal beings cannot be separated from their eternal welfare—the subjection of creatures to a fellow-creature cannot be separated from their subjection to their Creator,—and the power of their ruler to govern them cannot be separated from its source. All temporal welfare must be considered as subordinate to eternal welfare—all laws of man must be laid down in accordance with the law of

God—and every human ruler must, in his government, have regard to the rights of God.

If God has instituted among men a religious power to teach and to rule them with divine authority, in order to their eternal welfare and to the furtherance of His rights, it is clear that the civil ruler must take this religious power into account. He whose power is itself derived from God, cannot reasonably ignore a power which God has directly instituted, and the direct end of which is of its nature higher than is the direct end of his own power. He will have no right to make any law which is opposed to the law laid down with divine authority by that higher legislative power which is of God's own immediate institution,—and he will be bound not in any way to hinder the exercise of its religious authority. He will further be bound to lend his aid and to use the power at his disposal in support and defence of the religious society which God has created for the promotion of men's eternal welfare, and in strengthening the hands of the ruler of that society.

The two powers, the religious and the civil, are distinct, and each of them is in its own order independent. There is, nevertheless, in an exclusively Christian country a bond between the two powers, inasmuch as they are the same men who are the subjects of both powers. The two societies, the religious and the civil, are co-extensive.

The bond between them is not one of co-ordination, for the two powers are related to each other in the same way as the ends of those powers are related to each other. These ends are not co-ordinate, but subordinate the one to the other; the end of the civil power being the promotion of civil order and temporal welfare, while the end of the religious power is to secure God's rights and men's eternal welfare. But while there is, and—in the nature of things, and as reason itself demands—must be, subordination of the civil power to the religious power, this subordination is not of that kind which is called *direct*. Direct subordination of one power to another consists in this, that the subordinate power should, in matters which fall under its own proper end, be ruled by the superior power, and so be dependent on it in all its acts : and that the superior power should be able to annul, as well as to render valid, all acts of the subordinate power.

When Jesus Christ bestowed religious power on Peter, whom He made to be His Vicar for the teaching and ruling of that religious society which He founded, He did not bestow on him civil power over civil societies, or over civil rulers.

The ecclesiastical power has not therefore of itself care of the temporal welfare of mankind, which is the end of the civil power. In all those matters in which there is question only of temporal welfare, the civil power is independent. It is true that civil order conduces to religious order, but it is not therefore necessary that all the acts of the civil power should be regulated by the religious power. The order and welfare of the religious society demands indeed that the civil society should be rightly and justly governed; but it does not demand that the religious ruler should determine the mode of its government, and be the maker of all its laws, and the author of all its institutions.

The *indirect* subordination of the civil power to the religious power consists in this, that when the rights of God and the eternal welfare of human beings—the securing of which is the end of the religious power—demand it, the Vicar of Christ has the right, and it is his duty to direct the civil ruler in his exercise of the power which is entrusted to him for a lesser end, the temporal welfare of his subjects.

In all this there is no degradation of the civil power. Not only is there no imperfection in its dependence on the religious power, but it derives therefrom a perfection which it would not otherwise possess. Both powers are from God, but the things that are of God are rightly ordered, and it stands to reason that the lower power should be subordinate to the higher power, as are the things which are temporal to the things which are eternal, and as are the God-given rights of man to the inalienable rights of his Creator.

Such is the true conception of the relations of Church and State, to use a phrase which is in our day so often misunderstood, and as often misapplied. When these are observed, the ends of both powers are secured in the welfare, both temporal and eternal, of a Christian people.

2

When civil societies forget their Christian character, and lose sight of their Christian obligations, and vindicate for themselves independence of the religious power which God has established among them, and are bent on governing themselves as if Jesus Christ had no Vicar on this earth, they give rise to conflict. They place themselves in a position of antagonism to one who cannot abdicate and who cannot renounce the power which God has entrusted to him.

He who has the keys of the Kingdom of Heaven might in these unhappy circumstances exercise his authority to compel the submission of his subjects, under pain of loss of their rights of citizenship in the Kingdom of Christ. But with the compassion of a father he shrinks from proceeding to extremities with those who are still his children, and he strives to accommodate his government to their frailty, in so far as this may possibly be done without prejudice to rights which are not his own to dispose of at his will. Hence from time to time we find him entering into agreements with Christian princes, in which he lays down the limits beyond which it is not in his power to grant their desires, but within which he wills to gratify them by the concession of a privilege.

These agreements are not *contracts* between the Vicar of Christ on the one hand, and a Christian prince on the other. They are made not between equals, but between a superior and his subject. Every Christian prince or civil ruler is, as much as is the humblest of his Christian subjects, a member of that religious society which was instituted by Jesus Christ, and he is therefore a subject of the Vicar of Christ, who is the supreme ruler of that society.

The matter moreover of such agreements of its very nature excludes all idea of *contract*. Religious rights, or concerns which are bound up with religious rights, cannot be matter of contract between a divinely constituted and supreme religious ruler, and one of his own subjects.

The plenitude of religious power which belongs to the Vicar of Christ must always be preserved intact and whole as it was instituted by Christ in Peter. This does not demand that the whole of that power should be always and everywhere put forth in actual exercise, but it does demand that its possessor should be always free to exercise it, when it is, in his judgment, necessary or expedient for the common good that he should do so, and this independently of any consent on the part of any one of his subjects.

The Vicar of Christ is therefore free to exercise his judgment in the interests of Christ, and to refrain, under certain circumstances and during the continuance of these, from insisting on certain matters to which he has right—but he is not free to surrender his right of insisting if at any time he should deem it necessary or well to do so. This essential right he would be practically surrendering if he were to bind himself by any agreement which had the character of a contract. In a contract the obligation falls equally on each of the contracting parties, and it cannot be dissolved by either of them without the consent of the other. In a contract, moreover, both parties must be independent of each other, and free to contract, and the matter of the contract must be such as lies within the power of both one and the other.

In the agreements which the Vicar of Christ is free to make, and which from time to time he makes with Christian princes, there is no concession on the part of the prince. He is only paying that submission which he already owes as a subject to his religious ruler. There is a concession on the part of Christ's Vicar, at the instance of the prince, and the prince binds himself, not by way of contract, for contract there is none, but by way of solemn promise—superadded to his already existing obligation as a subject—to observe the terms of that concession, and to secure the observance of them by his subjects.

The interpretation of such agreements must be in accordance with their essential character. That of its very nature excludes all idea of contract, and so any phrases contained in them which if found in other agreements might imply contract, must not be interpreted in the sense of contract. Reason itself demands that this should be the law of the interpretation of such agreements.

Short of contract, however, and in addition to concession, there is in such phrases the expression of a true obligation on the part of the Vicar of Christ. He binds himself to fidelity in maintaining his concession so long as the privilege which he has granted is for the benefit of those in favour of whom he has given it, and is not detrimental to the general welfare of the Universal Church. This is a question which rests with him, however, to determine, since he is supreme ruler of all the faithful, and supreme judge of all questions of religion, both of faith and of morals. He is not only free to withdraw the privilege which he has granted, but he is in conscience bound to withdraw it if in his judgment he ought to do so.

By withdrawal of a privilege he is not imposing any burden in a new law, but simply recalling a portion of the flock to observance of certain details of the Common Law by which the Universal Church is governed. To the whole of that law all are bound, apart from special exemption by the Supreme Pastor.

Such is the true nature of the agreements between the Vicar of Christ and Christian princes, which are commonly known under the name of *Concordats*.

3

If God has established upon the earth a religious power for the securing of man's eternal welfare, it is clear, as we have seen, that civil power, which exists for the promotion only of man's temporal welfare, must be subordinate to religious power. It is clear also that, if the Incarnate Son of God has constituted one Supreme Head of all the members of the religious society which He founded, no civil ruler can possibly have right to hinder that freedom of intercourse between head and members therein, to which in every society both head and members are entitled. The Universal Church, which is the visible Kingdom of Christ, has its members in all kingdoms of the earth. These members form one body, of which the Vicar of Christ is the visible Head. As such it is his right and duty to exercise his immediate universal authority over every member of that body in every place of the whole earth. Every member has in turn the right to be ruled and governed by him in all matters which concern his eternal welfare. If this right of the religious subject is interfered with, he is deprived of his religious freedom.

If any civil ruler should declare that no utterance or act of religious authority made by the

Vicar of Christ should be of any force or avail within his dominions, apart from his permission, he would be arrogating to himself a power which God has not given him. He would be depriving his subjects of their religious freedom, and he would be inverting the divine order of the subordination of the temporal to the eternal, in making all exercise of religious power dependent on the civil power.

Such a claim on the part of a civil ruler would be equivalent to denial of the existence of any divinely established religious authority, and to assertion that the only supreme authority among men is that of the civil power which springs from the principles of nature—and that the only end of all authority is to promote man's temporal welfare.

Impatience of all religious control lies at the root of this claim. The reason on the surface of the claim is the pretended right to protect civil society from the aggressions and usurpations of ecclesiastical power. No wonder that the Vicar of Christ has always denounced this pretence as alike without foundation and as subversive of all ecclesiastical authority and order.

The anti-Christian character of the claim is manifest to all thinking men who believe that Jesus Christ is the Son of the living God—that as Man He is King of kings, and Lord of lords, and Prince of all rulers of the earth—that His royalty is not nominal, but real and actual, and that He not only reigns but rules and governs by means of that man whom He has made to be His Vicar on the earth—His Viceroy in His earthly Kingdom—and the Supreme Pastor of a flock which includes all the faithful, rulers as well as ruled, throughout the world.

The insult offered by this impious claim does not terminate in the Viceroy; it extends to his Sovereign Master, whom it implicitly impeaches as the founder of a power for the oppression of mankind—for the robbing of civil rulers of their rights—and for the disturbance, if not for the destruction of civil society.

The claim would be intelligible if it were made

by some pagan ruler who knows not Christ, but it is intellectually as well as morally unworthy of a Christian prince.

Such is the true character of that which is known in history as a royal *Placet* or *Exequatur*.

4

The Vicar of Christ has right to complete personal immunity, that is, to exemption from the jurisdiction of every civil ruler. This belongs to him by *divine law*, since it is essential to the free exercise of that supreme religious authority which is vested in him by divine institution. His immunity is not his own creation, and it is not by concession of the civil power—although he has embodied it in ecclesiastical law, and civil rulers have given to it the additional sanction of civil laws.

If the Vicar of Christ had not been already exempt by divine law from the jurisdiction of the civil power, he would have been subject thereto, and he could not by a law of his own have exempted himself therefrom. He who is once subject to an authority by law cannot by an act of his own will withdraw himself from the subjection which is due by him. There is nothing however to prevent the Vicar of Christ from making a law by which he authoritatively declares his already existing exemption by divine law, and by which he lays down the religious penalties which will be incurred by all who should interfere with the right which God has given him. This is the effect of the ecclesiastical laws which add the sanction of ecclesiastical penalties to the divine law of his immunity from all civil jurisdiction.

When civil rulers have similarly lent the sanction of their civil laws to this divine law, it is because, although they have no power to abrogate that which they did not create, they could by means of physical force hinder the exercise of a divine right. By their laws they undertake not only to abstain from all invasion of this divine right, but to support and defend it by means of the physical force which is at their command. Such civil laws have the true idea of laws, so far as the subjects of these rulers are concerned, whom they can compel by means of those laws, and the penalties which they attach to the transgression of them, to respect the divine law which they thus embody in their civil code. They do not create the right which they recognize as already existing, and as divine, when they fulfil their duty as Christian princes by legislating in support of the Church of Christ.

In pagan countries where Christ is not known, the rights of His Vicar cannot be recognized, and the exercise of them is both liable and likely to be hindered by physical force. But hindrance of the exercise of a right does not negative the existence of the right itself. This was the case during the first centuries and before the conversion of civil rulers to Christianity. Actual immunity from civil jurisdiction was not then enjoyed by the Vicar of Christ, but he had all along and from the beginning that divine right to it which was inherent in his divinely instituted office. To the perfect fulfilment of that office this right is essential, and it is as essential to the perfect welfare of those for whose spiritual benefit that office exists.

The immunity of a supreme religious ruler is essential to the very idea of a Universal Church. Every member of a world-wide society has the same right to be unhindered and free to be ruled immediately by its supreme ruler, as that ruler has to his unhindered freedom in ruling every one of his subjects. The freedom of the Church of Christ is bound up with the freedom of the Vicar of Christ.

This freedom must be *stable*, and it must moreover be *manifest* to the whole world. It must not be dependent on the changeable will of man, and the reality of it must be placed beyond suspicion.

If the Vicar of Christ had his dwelling within the dominions of a civil ruler who acknowledged his divine independence of all civil jurisdiction, he would have actual exercise of his right of immunity, along with recognition of that right. He would however have no other guarantee for the continuance of either, than the piety of that prince, and his perseverance in his piety.

He would, moreover, even while really free from civil jurisdiction, have the appearance of being subject to it. The reason why men are the subjects of a particular prince is that they are dwelling within his dominions, and if the Vicar of Christ had his habitual dwelling in the dominions of some prince, he would—however really independent, and known to be so by his fellow-citizens —come to be regarded by men of other nations as practically the subject of that prince. In addition to this, his exemption would always have the appearance of a concession, or privilege granted by, and dependent on the will of the prince in whose territory he was living, and whose subject, apart from exemption, he would naturally have been.

Under the most favourable circumstances the impartiality of the Vicar of Christ would be liable to suspicion in the minds of other princes and of other peoples, and especially if, in the fulfilment of his duty he had to prescribe a course of conduct which was distasteful to them from the point of view of their national interest, or temporal welfare. They might then, and not unnaturally, suspect that his action was not spontaneous and unbiassed—that he had been either led by partiality, or driven by force. There is only one way in which his independence of all jurisdiction of any civil power can be put at once on a stable basis and beyond suspicion, and that is his territorial isolation, with possession of civil princedom, and recognition of him as a sovereign prince by other civil rulers.

An institution is to be referred to the action of Divine providence, which when brought about by the course of events, is manifestly the most efficacious means towards an end which is known with certainty to have been intended by God. Such an end is the independence of the Vicar of Christ from all civil jurisdiction, since this independence is inherent in his office, and essential to the exercise of his universal religious authority. His civil princedom gradually grew up from the date of the conversion of civil rulers to Christianity, and therefore as soon as its existence became physically possible. It matured with the growth of Christendom, and it has never been interfered with without grievous damage to the Church of Christ.

The right of the Vicar of Christ to civil princedom—as it is a means, and the chief means, and practically the only adequate means for securing his independence—is distinct from his other right to dominion over territories which belong to him by the same title which gives right to other lawful owners of their possessions. When he is deprived of these territories he is robbed of his property, but when he is deprived of his civil princedom, he is divested of his personal independence and official freedom.

The question is not a national one, to be determined in the interest, or by the temporal interests

of one nation. It is of cosmopolitan concern.
There is no nation which has not a vested interest
in the territorial independence of the supreme and
immediate religious teacher and ruler of all Christian men throughout the world.

Throughout the centuries of conflict between the
Roman Pontiffs and the rulers of this world, and
amidst all the variety of character to be observed
in the men who have sat successively on the
throne of Peter, there is one characteristic which
we find to be common to them all. In every one
of them is apparent the same abiding consciousness
of what he is—and of what he is not—that he is
the Vicar of Jesus Christ—and that he is only the
Vicar of Jesus Christ—and that therefore it is not
within his power to surrender one single right
which has been entrusted to him. The *Non possumus* of the Pontiffs is the clearest expression of the
plenitude of their power, as they are Viceroys of
the King of kings.

In his successors Peter perseveres in his See, and

their consciousness of what they are is as abiding as is the consciousness of one man of that which he individually is. It rests on Christ's words of promise, and the words whereby He fulfilled His promise, for to every one and to all of them collectively, as with Peter they form one moral person, did Jesus speak when he said to Simon of Bethsaida, " I say to thee that thou art Peter, and on this Rock I will build My Church—I will give to thee the keys of the Kingdom of Heaven— Confirm thy brethren—Feed My sheep." The interpretation of a promise is found in its fulfilment, and the words of Christ are verified in the existence of His Vicar.

The children of this world may cry aloud, "We will not have this man to reign over us; we have no king save Cæsar;" but the Cæsars of this world are stricken as by an unseen hand when they enter into conflict with that Church against which the gates of Hell are powerless to prevail.

History repeats itself in recording the imprisonments, the spoliations, and the martyrdoms of the Vicars of the Crucified, but it has also to bear its testimony to the resurrections to freedom and to exercise of right of the Vicars of the Risen. The contest is as unequal as the issue is inevitable On the one side is the physical force of civil power, but on the other is the strength, made perfect in weakness, of that power to which the civil power is subordinated by the ordinance of Him from whom it is derived. "Understand, O ye kings," cried the Psalmist in prophetic vision, "receive instruction, you that are judges of the earth. The kings of the earth stood up, and the princes took counsel together against the Lord, and against His Christ. But He that dwelleth in the heavens shall laugh at them, and the Lord shall have them in derision."

Given that Jesus is the Christ of the Lord, the Incarnate Son of the living God, and that He has associated and morally identified His Vicar with Himself, as He is the living Rock, the foundation and corner-stone of the one Catholic and Roman Church, need we wonder at the tale that history has to tell of the final issue of every attack made by princes on the Roman Pontiffs? The assailants of a viceroy are assailants of his sovereign, and the words which Christ said of Himself extend to His Vicar: "The stone which the builders rejected, the same is become the head of the corner. Whosoever shall fall on this stone shall be broken, and on whomsoever it shall fall it shall grind him to powder."

www.ingramcontent.com/pod-product-compliance
Lightning Source LLC
Chambersburg PA
CBHW031402160426
43196CB00007B/864